MY DOG WON'T STOP BARKING!

Discover the Secrets to Stop Your Dog Barking…

…and Barking…

…and Barking…

Chris Morris

All Rights Reserved

No part of this publication may be reproduced in any form or by any means, including scanning, photocopying, or otherwise without prior written permission of the copyright holder. Copyright © 2013

Disclaimer and Terms of Use

By reading this book, you assume all risks associated with using the advice given below, with a full understanding that you, solely, are responsible for anything that may occur as a result of putting this information into action in any way, and regardless of your interpretation of the advice.

You are given a non-transferable "personal use" licence to this book. You cannot distribute it or share it with other individuals.

Also, there are no resale rights or private label rights granted when purchasing this book. It is for your personal use only.

A Note on Pronouns!

Throughout this book I have used the pronouns *he, him* or *his* in every instance, purely for the sake of being consistent. I know that your dog is very likely to be female, and in that case please imagine that the word reads *she, her* or *hers*. If there is a strong enough demand I will produce a separate version for owners of female dogs to choose instead!

Copyright: Chris Morris © 2013
ISBN 9781470105686

Contents

1. Why Is My Dog Barking? — 1
2. Barking Prevention — 6
3. Training Methods — 11
4. Early Training - The Puppy Dog — 14
5. When the Doorbell Rings — 18
6. When a Guest or Visitor Comes to the House — 21
7. When A Dog Is Left Alone — 24
8. When Someone Approaches Or Passes The House — 28
9. Anti-Barking Collars — 31
10. Dogmas — 33
11. Dog Breed Barking Characteristics — 36
12. The Aftermath: Like A Dog With Two Tails! — 38
13. Photo Acknowledgements — 40

1. Why Is My Dog Barking?

© Nazreth

Your dog is barking. He is barking a lot, too much in fact. It is only natural for a dog to bark though, isn't it?

However, if your dog is barking excessively, uncontrollably even, then this is not desirable and can affect your life, the way you do things, your relationship with your neighbors and possibly with your friends. This does need to be resolved, and I will show you how.

In these pages you will discover how to control your dog's barking, and that there is no need to feel dominated by your dog's behavior, whether consciously or sub-consciously. Not only will you gain full mastery over your dog and his behavior but you will also have the satisfaction of knowing that you have achieved this yourself. Your friends and neighbors will admire your ability to overcome a problem which many people are totally unable to find an answer to, and you will also establish yourself as the sort of person who confronts an issue and finds a solution to it.

Once you have applied the principles in this book you will have the satisfaction and confidence of knowing that you have the ability to control your dog's barking in any situation. You will no longer feel helpless in your efforts to gain obedience from your dog. That is not to say that you would ever desire to have a tyrannical hold over a dog's natural instincts, but these subtle techniques will ensure that the power is there within you, and your dog will understand that.

The first thing you need to consider is the cause, or causes, of your dog's barking behavior. A dog's bark is only his natural voice, after all, but just as there are as many as 39 different nuances to a dog's vocal expressions, there are many different intensities and frequencies to take into account on the scale between normal barking and excessive barking. Fundamentally, we need to identify the underlying cause.

There are so many things to bark about… © Lilyz Studio

So what are the reasons why a dog may bark in a constantly recurring cycle? You won't be surprised to know that there are many driving forces, beyond the obvious instinct to bark as an alarm or warning, out of fear from a perceived threat, be it another dog or a human, and also from sheer excitement.

A dog's bark is a means of expression after all, and he may do so because he is bored, anxious or highly strung, because he is frustrated, or perhaps at a loud noise or repeated noises. He may bark as an attention-seeking device, or for territorial reasons.

A dog which is left alone for long periods may bark out of loneliness, or to call his owner back home. Of course there are also the obvious reasons, such as physical discomfort, whether too hot, too cold, hungry, or simply feeling ill – and in an older dog it could be out of crankiness, confusion, or even some form of dog dementia. Or it could simply be to say hello.

That is not an exhaustive list, but it does illustrate the different occasions or circumstances which may lead a dog to bark, and then perhaps not to cease barking for a long time. You first need to identify the underlying cause for your dog's persistent barking. Perhaps you could keep a log of your dog's exact environment and any external factors which appear to trigger off his noisy barking.

So we have established that a dog will normally bark for a specific reason. There may be a number of reasons why he will bark at different times, but the persistent, uncontrollable barking is the pattern which should be identified at this stage.

Here is a list of some occasions which can cause a dog to bark. Take a look to identify any underlying reasons which may relate to your pet's behavior.

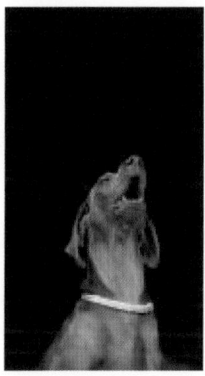

© Lilyz Studio

- Barking due to Alarm (territorial, fear)
- Barking due to Anxiety
- Barking due to Attention seeking
- Barking due to Boredom
- Barking due to Cold (physical discomfort)

- Barking due to Confusion (elderly dog)
- Barking due to Dementia (elderly dog)
- Barking due to Dominance Assertion
- Barking at the Doorbell (noise)
- Barking due to a dog's Environment (physical discomfort, boredom, noise)
- Barking due to Excitement
- Barking due to Fear
- Barking due to Frustration (boredom, inactivity)
- Barking as a Greeting (excitement)
- Barking at Guests (territorial, excitement)
- Barking for Health reasons (physical discomfort)
- Barking due to being Highly Strung (anxiety, excitement)
- Barking due to feeling Hot (physical discomfort)
- Barking due to Hunger (physical discomfort)
- Barking due to Inactivity (boredom)
- Barking due to being left Alone (boredom, lonely)
- Barking due to Loneliness (left alone, boredom)
- Barking due to Noise
- Barking due to Old Age
- Barking at Other Dogs (territorial, fear)
- Barking due to Physical Discomfort
- Barking at Strangers (territorial)
- Territorial Barking

- Barking in response to a Threat (alarm, fear)

- Barking at Visitors (territorial, excitement)

By now you should have identified the types of occasion and a pattern of behavior which precedes or accompanies your dog's incessant barking, and armed with this knowledge it is now a matter of removing the cause or causes. If this is not possible because of your particular circumstances, such as having to leave your dog alone for long periods when you go to work, or a recurring loud noise in the local area for example, it is still possible either to use a relevant form of training, or to use some lateral thinking to alleviate the problem.

You will find many different sets of circumstances which are described throughout this book, and although yours may not be an identical match with any of them, it is almost certain that you will find some reference points to your own individual problem as you read further.

2. Barking Prevention

The events which may cause your dog to bark can be loosely divided into three main categories. In this chapter I will set out to show you a method which will enable you to prevent or modify the conditions which regularly occur that are most likely to cause your dog to bark excessively. You will not need to worry about this seemingly insurmountable problem once you have the knowledge to identify and control your dog's apparently insatiable demand for noise of his own making!

So your dog will feel more contented within a better environment for both himself and his owner, and you can cease worrying that he may set off barking at any moment. Read right through this chapter and you will feel a sense of enlightenment and an 'aha' moment as you do. No more desperate seeking of quick cures, you will now grasp the principles and be able to apply them directly to the root of the problem.

The first point to understand is that your dog will be inclined to bark when a situation arises in which he finds it more rewarding to bark than it is to be silent. If you remove your dog from that situation, or change the situation itself, and at the same time make it more rewarding for the dog to be quiet than it is to bark, what do you think he will do?

I mentioned earlier that three underlying categories will be a trigger point for a dog to bark. The commonest instances are when a dog is left alone, when a dog is affected by the approach of visitors or strangers (including passers-by), and a dog will also bark to gain the attention he feels he is not receiving.

At no stage would we wish to stop your dog from barking completely, and it is only when a dog does not know when to stop that there is cause for concern. You do not want to make a fundamental change in your dog's character after all. However, excessive barking is almost always related to an underlying issue, and the cause is usually behavioral.

Here is an example of a dog barking because he needs something that he isn't getting, and how to correct the situation:

Your dog is not getting enough exercise, and has too much pent-up energy. He is barking madly to burn off some of this energy. If he is under-exercised the obvious solution, once identified, is to keep your dog active; and if he is not receiving enough mental stimulation he will be mentally under-exercised (bored!), so try to engage him more fully. Such physical and mental stimulation can in themselves be enough to reduce his barking, both in frequency and in volume. A tired dog is far more likely to be a quiet dog.

I'm going to be tired after all this running around © Asia Jones

Another reason for barking could be some incorrect behavior which has been reinforced in your dog in the past, which needs to be corrected to remove the cause. An example of this is to comfort a dog when he is barking to gain attention. By rewarding your dog, petting him or giving him a treat to quieten his barking, you are giving in to his demands and sending him the message that this 'incorrect behavior' works just fine. Instead you should just ignore him, and then reward him when he has become quiet. This will form an association in his mind that he gains a reward for 'correct behavior', if only he knew what that was!

These are simple examples which may very well not match your own circumstances, but the important principle is to identify the cause, then be consistent in the way you deal with this. Persistence and consistency of proven methods will eventually pay off.

We will now follow this through from beginning to end with a specific example of what to do in a given situation, and you may be able to transpose this to your own. If not, there are some more detailed examples of different situations in later chapters.

THE PROBLEM

I have a particular issue with my dog. He barks quite normally most of the time, but he sets off on an uncontrollable bout of incessant loud barking from time to time. I have no idea why, but I am going to look into it. As far as I can tell he only ever seems to do this whenever he sees a delivery vehicle or a bus, and even more so when the people inside them get out and pass the house. If a dog passes by, particularly without its owner, then he will bark and make more fuss than ever.

What am I going to do? I have read a magazine article somewhere and I think this may be called territorial barking, but the problem is that I am unable to stop him barking once he has been triggered by these external events. Perhaps I should seek out some professional training for my dog to stop him doing this and annoying the neighbors, but I can't really afford it.

Woof © Sue Byford

I have found this book which suggests some solutions to incessant barking in nearly all circumstances, and there may be a particular solution for my problem. Aha, here it is. I should remove the physical cues which set him off barking.

What does that mean, I can't stop the traffic and all these people moving backwards and forwards past my flat? Just a minute, it says here that I should remove my dog from the cause of the barking, so I must put him in the back of the house to stop him seeing what is going on outside. Great! I only have a flat, just the one room, and I'm not going to move. But I can put up some net curtains and see if that does the trick. I'll give it a week to see if that works, then if it doesn't I guess I will have to draw the curtains most of the day, or put him in the bedroom during the day as a last resort.

At least then I will be able to measure the success of this solution and take it step by step to the goal I have in mind, which is peace and quiet and friendlier neighbors.

OK, so perhaps that is a little simplistic, even though it is a common everyday occurrence for thousands of dog owners, but you get the idea. Identify the cause; seek out and evaluate a remedy; apply this directly to your situation, with small amendments if necessary; try to find a way of measuring the success of this solution; carry it out consistently and persistently; wait for the right result.

It is important not to rush or be impatient with whichever technique you choose as the best one for your circumstances. Begin with a simple exercise, and introduce your dog slowly to the method. If time is available, steadily spend a little longer each time you carry out the method, but above all it is important to be regular and consistent. You may feel that it is not working at all at first, but as with so many things, if you are persistent and keep at it then you will finally see the result that makes the effort worthwhile.

It is a good idea to set aside a certain period each day to carry out the method, and try hard not to miss a day. If you are going on holiday quite shortly, for example, it would probably be best to delay the start altogether – but don't use this as an excuse to procrastinate! There is always something going on or about to happen, isn't there?

Be thoroughly prepared before you start, 'manufacture' the opportunity, and know what to do next. If you wait for the right 'natural' opportunity to arise then you may not be fully prepared, and your dog may already have reacted to the event and will probably be difficult to stop at an early stage of the training. It is best if your dog is calm, receptive, and ready to take on his behavioral shift.

During the course of your training methods it is a good idea to listen out for any unsolicited comments about your dog's barking behavior from friends, family or neighbors, especially if they are unaware of what you have undertaken. You could always ask a pertinent question if no comments are forthcoming, but then you will have to gauge the value of the comment accordingly. People normally like to be polite!

You can also gain some 'comment' from your dog, in his attitude and general behavior. Does he seem happy, does he think it is all a game? You don't want to stress him out, but that is more likely if you don't undertake any of these methods – yelling at a dog to be quiet just reinforces the dog's desire to speak in a loud voice. I am sure you don't do that anyway, do you?

Take on board any valid comments you receive from humans or from your dog, and in the light of your own observations as well it is perfectly fine to adapt any methods a little if necessary. You know your dog and your situation best. The important thing is to carry it out right through to the end, and await the desired result.

3. Training Methods

Barking on Command

Now that you have some ideas about the types of preventative measures which you can take in future to negate your dog's incessant barking, you can take an important step by learning how to teach your dog to bark when you ask him to and, more importantly, to stop barking when you say so. This is sometimes known as Barking on Command, or Speak and Be Quiet Training, and these methods will allow you to exercise ultimate control over your dog.

The techniques which you are about to learn will prevent you from losing control of your dog's barking ever again and, once learned, this mutual training will help you to guide your dog's behavior in other areas which may be necessary. The loss of control which you may now feel is becoming overwhelming can be turned around within a few short weeks, and both you and your dog will have mutual respect for each other and this joint achievement. No more yelling at the dog to stop barking, that belongs to yesterday.

The concept of telling your dog to bark on command may seem contrary at first. After all, it is the precise opposite of your overriding intentions, which are to find ways of stopping him barking. Nevertheless, although this technique is often overlooked, it has been proven to be one of the easiest and best methods of curing excessive barking for good.

The emphasis of this technique is to form an association between your dog's actions, in this case barking, and the words which you speak, followed by a reward. This is intended to reinforce the sequence of events in your dog's mind.

I can bark if you want © Lejla Alic

Here is a step by step plan which you should follow for as long as is necessary. The training can take place for 10 or 15 minutes each day, once or twice a day if possible, and you should plan to act out these steps consistently over several weeks.

First of all, decide on which word you will use to command your dog to bark. No need to make this complicated, a simple 'bark' or 'speak' or 'talk' will do. Then of course you will also require a different word for the command to stop barking. Another straightforward word will do – perhaps 'enough', or 'hush' or 'quiet'.

You will also need ready access to some particularly tasty rewards to give your dog, whatever his favorite treat is. Try to avoid giving him this treat on other occasions, particularly for the duration of the training. The decision over whether you wish to start with the 'bark' command or the 'quiet' command is variable, and it really depends on you knowing your dog, and the level and persistence of his barking.

It is in fact perfectly possible to train your dog with both commands at the same time. After all, each time your dog barks he will also stop barking at some point. It is the association of this occurring at the same time as your command, and your dog's identification of this specific reward for doing so which is important. Again, it will depend on your dog, and you know your dog best.

Let's start with the 'quiet' command. Wait for an occasion when your dog is barking for some reason, and then gain his attention with a whistle or a clap. He will probably stop barking at this point, out of surprise or interest at what you are up to, and immediately he stops barking speak your 'command' word in a firm, positive voice, so he knows that you mean it.

Simultaneously give your dog the treat which you have ready, a good reason in itself why he will not start barking again. Now repeat this process often, but don't overdo it, and do make sure you keep each session brief.

Be prepared for this to take several weeks to accomplish. When your dog has mastered this command, if you are training him with each command separately, then now is the time to take on the 'bark' training. You should already have a better understanding of each other after carrying out the first command, and this second stage may well be easier.

First of all you should contrive a situation which you know will always lead to your dog barking. It is best if this is a situation that you can control, such as a ring on the doorbell or the telephone ringing, rather than waiting for the occasion to arise randomly. This is because you need to be aware that your dog is just about to bark, and immediately before he does so you will say your 'bark' command in a clear and positive voice.

When your dog has barked three or four times you will respond positively by saying 'good bark', 'good speak', whatever is your chosen barking command. Simultaneously reward your dog with a treat, which will very likely stop him barking immediately.

As with the first stage of training, it may take many repetitions of this before your dog fully understands the association between your command and his barking, but it will happen. When you are confident that your dog is trained to respond to both commands, you should practise them both together, in the form 'speak' ('bark', etc.) and 'quiet' ('hush', etc.).

Your patience and consistency will have been rewarded, and so will your dog – many times over!

4. Early Training - The Puppy Dog

© Dani Gi

Of course a puppy does not bark excessively, he may barely bark at all, but puppyhood is a good time to engender in your puppy some confidence in being alone. A puppy which is too strongly bonded to his owner will become a dog which will not be left alone without making an enormous fuss.

This training over the next few pages will ensure that a puppy is comfortable with himself, and does not become overly dependent upon you. It is unlikely that you can be there all the time, and sooner or later he will have to know how to amuse himself on his own.

The adult dog will be much easier to control by using these early training techniques, which are gentle in themselves but prevent more radical action being necessary in years to come. Both you and your puppy will have an inherent understanding of each other's standpoint after carrying out a few basic principles which will prevent him from being an anxious dog who may well become an excessive barker.

Fundamentally, this training sets out to ensure that a puppy does not bark when left alone or feel that he needs attention. The puppy will soon learn to be contented when he is away from you, secure in the knowledge that you will return to look after him. If he is with you all the time, he will become overly anxious when you are not there.

The training should start when your puppy is around nine or ten weeks old. Obviously he will fuss and make a lot of noise when he is playing and the point of this exercise is never to stop a dog's natural noise and flamboyance. It is purely to discourage him from barking for attention, and to stop him 'training' you to react to his every whim.

What's wrong with my natural noise and flamboyance? © Aokiharu

At all stages during this training you should of course be aware that a puppy has many requirements, not the least of which is hunger, so this is not to suggest that you ignore all of his barks if there is an obvious need.

However, if the puppy is barking or fussing to gain your attention persistently, even annoyingly, there is nothing to be gained by responding to this with a simple 'hush', still worse to respond positively by petting him. The best reaction is to get up and leave the room without comment, thus teaching your puppy that you do not respond to his attention seeking.

You do not come to him on demand. Just a few weeks of this procedure will easily demonstrate to the puppy that barking long enough and loud enough does not work. This gentle reinforcement of behavior is all that is required, as long as it is made obvious and consistent.

Please play with me © Dimitri Castrique

You will very likely feel guilty for ignoring your puppy at times, as every natural instinct tells you to comfort the young dog. After all, he will have been removed from his mother while very young and he is bound to want attention. This should be given at all times, except for the times when he demands it. His puppy barks will become much louder barks as an adult, and it is vital that this behavioral pattern is discouraged.

There are several ways that you can help your puppy to feel contented and be happy with his own company right from the start. For example, a good idea for comforting your puppy when he is alone can be something as simple as placing a loud ticking clock in the room. This may remind the puppy of his mother's heartbeat, and the calming effect of his association of your absence with the soothing, regular sound of a ticking clock will be quite likely to instill a sense of wellbeing, contented with his own company in quiet surroundings. Another example of a soothing noise could also be some quiet radio or television in the background, offering some cozy companionship while you are gone.

This may not always work as well in reality as it sounds on paper, so an alternative may be to record your own voice speaking soothingly and quietly, then put it on a loop; you could also try leaving your scent behind on a pile of clothes in the corner, or ideally in his bed. Now you have an excuse not to wash your clothes so often!

His own space, ideally a bed - not your bed - or a regular spot where he is happy to be, can be the place where your puppy is used to having his toys and little treats, and the place where he will feel 'at home' at home, even when you are not there. If he can amuse himself on his own, in his own pad, your absence will be missed all the less, and he will not grow up to be an anxious, insecure dog who is constantly barking to call you home, and calling the neighbors round to complain when you do get home...

Somewhere I can feel relaxed and contented © Mariana Figueroa

5. When the Doorbell Rings...

The obvious solution is to change your doorbell – especially if you have one like ours which can sound like a barking dog! However, this is too simplistic of course, and simply changing your doorbell to a knocker is very unlikely to prevent your dog from barking at the noise. Anything is worth a try, but in reality it is a noise, rather than the noise, which is the only stimulus a dog may need to set off barking incessantly.

A method you may want to try is known as "flooding". The simple procedure is to embark on a training program which convinces your dog that the noise from the door, be it a bell or a knock, does not equate to visitors, and hence some excitement for the day.

Was that the doorbell? © wookiee

So using this technique, you ring the doorbell yourself very frequently, so that the dog becomes used to the noise, and ceases to associate it with anybody standing on the doorstep for him to greet, or guard his territory against.

Perhaps this may not be subtle enough for your clever dog, and he may see through your little scheme. If so, a similar idea is to change your dog's perspective of the doorbell.

If he associates it with something other than, better than, barking and rushing at the door, then he will become conditioned to respond in an entirely different way.

Who keeps ringing that doorbell? I'm trying to sleep! © Macej

So, for example, if you give your dog a lot of attention each time the doorbell rings, perhaps tossing a ball in the air for him to catch, or maybe giving him a favorite treat, then in future when he hears the doorbell ring he will associate it with something that he enjoys, a game or a treat. Something not to be barked at!

This is entirely different to rewarding your dog for barking. What you are doing through this technique is to condition your dog so that he associates the doorbell with something enjoyable, and not as an occasion for barking.

6. When a Guest or Visitor Comes to the House...

There are a variety of reasons why a family dog may bark at a visitor. He may be afraid, or be aggressive out of a territorial motivation, or simply be excited that something new is happening. You should recognize here that it is of course perfectly normal for your dog to bark at the approach of a 'stranger' to the house. He is warning of a possible danger to himself and the 'pack', and he will normally cease such territorial barking when the leader of the 'pack' (i.e. you) arrives to take charge. A problem only arises here if the dog continues to bark when you are present. He is very likely to be showing through this behavior that he believes he has the dominant role in the 'pack'. You need to re-establish the owner-dog relationship in order for your dog to know who is in charge here!

However, it may also be the case that your dog is barking through fear, rather than territorially. This is most apparent if he should dart to and fro towards your visitor, or retreat and bark from a little further away.

The most important aspect of this training method is to change your dog's perspective of visitors. He should recognize them as being not only welcome within the house but also as a positive pleasure. This is accomplished by a form of positive reinforcement, and these are the steps you could take.

Firstly, to set the scene correctly for the training you should leave the dog in a different room so that the guest is free to sit down without interference.

The next step is to have some of your dog's favorite treats handy, without him first having seen them in the room. These should then be strewn around the floor at your visitor's feet, a welcoming sight for any dog.

Once your dog has settled in the separate room let him wander into the room where the guest is sitting, but be careful not make eye contact with your dog or acknowledge him in any way. He will find the treats himself and be contented at your visitor's feet. This will establish an association between your guest and having his favorite treat, and although he will be very likely to react by barking in the normal way on the next occasion you have a visitor, this training technique will work if repeated often enough. Better still with many different guests on several different occasions - if you are that popular!

Your dog should now recognize a visitor standing outside the door as someone who brings treats, not as a threat. Obviously this is not the mild reaction you would want from a guard dog, but we are talking of family pets here. An additional reinforcement or variation of this technique would be for a guest to enter your home carrying one of your dog's favorite toys which will have been left just outside the front door.

This is particularly useful if the dog is then distracted by having the toy placed in his mouth. He will now be unable to bark and, if the toy is a well-chosen favorite then he will prefer to have it in his mouth than bark anyway. Again, the message sent to your dog by this method is that a visitor is welcome to the house, and is positively associated with a toy rather than as an occasion for barking.

If you are not in the habit of entertaining guests at your house regularly, then it would be more appropriate to adopt a different technique altogether, since it is not possible to positively reinforce the 'welcome visitor' training when there is too great an interval between visits.

The most suitable method in this instance is that your dog will be separated from your visitor as referred to above. On this occasion though, he must stay there until your guest is ready to leave, and then you may open the door and settle your dog down to sit quietly with a treat as your guest leaves. The form of repetitive behavioral training necessary to establish a proper dog-visitor relationship cannot be maintained without regular visitors, and this is a fairly unsatisfactory yet reliable solution.

7. When A Dog Is Left Alone...

I have previously dealt in an earlier chapter with the training of a young dog to be content with his own company, and thus not to set him up for barking to call you home when he grows older. However, if you are already past the stage of early training then a consistent reinforcement technique is called for.

A dog which barks excessively when he has been left alone is an insecure dog. He is conditioned to his owner doting on his every whim, and he needs to learn how to be alone. This can be a painful experience if you have what may be termed an overly close relationship, but if he feels abandoned without you then you have two choices. Be with him all the time, or develop a strategy for him to feel settled and contented in your absence.

From the dog's point of view, if he barks persistently when you have left the house and then eventually you return (as you will, of course), his impression will be that his barking to call you home has been successful. It has brought about the result he wanted from the start, and he will continue to do so in the future. Even worse, if you rush back home as soon as you hear him barking you are firmly reinforcing this idea.

The first point to bear in mind with this training is to appreciate that a dog will respond to your body language rather than to your words. The only words he will respond to directly should be command words, if you have already trained him to react to these.

However, your body language can demonstrate a great deal to a dog, so in the first instance you must refrain from any form of reassurance that you will 'be back soon' accompanied by a lot of petting. This will have precisely the opposite of the effect intended, and will create anxiety in your dog. Will he ever see you again? Can he come too?

Rule out any emphasis on your departure whatsoever. First of all make sure that your dog is settled happily with a chew or a favorite toy; then simply leave without comment. You must establish in your dog's mind that your coming and going from the house is totally unremarkable. If you do not remark on your departure or return in the slightest, then your dog will come to recognize that this is 'no big deal' after all.

Naturally you should begin this training by creating very short absences and gradually increasing the length of absence. It would be best if you return from your first absence before your dog becomes agitated, and to continue this pattern over increased periods of time. Upon your return each time, it is very important that you enter the house as calmly and quietly as you left, and resume whatever you were doing before you left.

Difficult though it may be at first, you should ignore your dog totally, even if he is wildly excited, and make no eye contact whatsoever. The dog must believe that your absence was no big deal for you, so why should it be a big deal for him.

After a short period of 'settling in' at home, look at your dog to acknowledge him, and give a familiar command if possible. 'Sit' would be a good one to use if your dog responds well to that. It should only be after he has responded to this command that the reward comes.

A good pat, a friendly reassurance that he is a good dog, or a familiar expression, and then you are back to normal. Nothing much has happened. You left, you came back.

A development of this technique when you are ready to leave your dog for a whole day is to prepare him for your departure with some recognizable signals. For example, you can make ready to leave in the normal way, which you can be sure your dog is very likely to notice.

Then you will continue with some small task around the house, ignoring your dog as you do so. Shortly afterwards you can calmly walk away from the room without looking at your dog or saying anything. By now your dog will be fully prepared for your departure and will be settled with his chew or favorite toy. Repeat the process of calmly re-entering the house when you return.

Something to chew on © cookai

Naturally, you would wish your dog to be as contented as possible during your absence, so it is a good idea to leave your dog's favorite things close by. Perhaps some dry food could be left in different places around the house for him to discover during the day. You could hide this within a Kong toy perhaps.

You know what your dog likes best, and if he responds well to the radio or television then a little quiet background noise would be comforting, particularly if your house is rarely totally silent when you are there.

Hidden Treasures © Kathyra1

The important thing to remember is that your dog will definitely be aware of your departure, and it does seem rude in human terms to ignore him and not to say goodbye as we leave. However, the only way to ensure that your dog is not overly distraught with separation anxiety is to convince him that your coming and going passes without comment, and he will adjust to this in time. Above all, be consistent!

8. When Someone Approaches Or Passes The House...

Territorial Barking

The most obvious way of preventing this recurring problem is to remove the problem. As it is not possible to remove either vehicles or people passing by in the street outside, the next best solution is to remove your dog from the problem.

This is easily done if he is no longer allowed in the particular room where he can see or hear all the outside activity. Alternatively, you could close the curtains when your dog is in the room. A more labor-intensive solution would be to erect a high fence or grow a tall hedge.

Again, if your dog barks without let up after the postman has done his daily round then the easy answer is to remove your dog from the area near your front door. If your dog is normally outside the front of the house, just put him out the back.

If you can, try to see things from your dog's point of view, think how you would be affected by the external activity, and come up with a different way of doing things so that you – or your dog – are no longer affected by them.

Is that the mail man again? He seems to come every day! © Daniel Andrés Forero

For example, you dog may be outdoors a lot, but be consistently disturbed by some noises beyond your property. He may be unable to see what is making the noise, and this may worry him.

If it is at all possible, you could find a way of him seeing where the noise is coming from. If you have a fence that you could put a couple of small holes in at his head height then he can take a look, and this will quite likely reassure him that there is nothing to be concerned about. Possibly!

What's going on out there? © Ned Horton

Barking excessively at any external disturbance may have such a relatively simple solution, but it is also possible that your dog may be barking to protect his territory. This is normal to some degree, and it only becomes a problem when the barking continues long after the 'threat' has disappeared.

This could indicate that your dog is over-anxious, and perhaps sees himself as the 'alpha' dog, with responsibility to guard the whole pack. In this instance you must make sure that he becomes firmly aware that you take the dominant role in the pack, and that it is up to you, rather than him, to guard the house.

9. Anti-Barking Collars

I would strongly advocate that you persevere with all the various training techniques outlined in this book before considering different forms of action. In most cases you just need time and a consistent application of these methods before the desired result will be achieved. It would be true to say, however, that not all methods will work on all dogs in all circumstances, given that you and your dog have individual relationships and each and every one is subtly different in some way.

There are several types of anti-barking collars available, and although I would consider these to be a last resort, it would be foolish to dismiss their usefulness out of hand. Electric shock collars are certainly not going to be considered in these pages, indeed they are banned in many countries.

Other, less extreme, deterrent collars can be useful in certain circumstances however, and there are two in particular which I will discuss here.

Ultrasonic Anti-Barking Collars are primarily for outdoor use, and the principle is based on a dog's high-frequency hearing, which will cause your dog to be distracted when he hears this ultra high-pitched sound. This form of 'training' is designed to make your dog cease barking whenever he hears this rather unpleasant sound.

This contradicts most of the techniques which you will have read through this book, being based rather on the stick than the carrot, of course. Nevertheless, the sound does not hurt your dog, and his association of this high-pitched noise with his barking is likely to have some sort of deterrent effect.

You should always bear in mind that a dog's bark is a natural response to his surroundings, and his expression of how he is feeling at the time, and no owner would wish for their dog's outgoing personality to be affected. It is important to understand that collars such as this, and the citronella spray collar, are primarily intended for short-term use to solve an extreme barking problem, and not to deny your dog his bark altogether!

The Citronella Collar is a spray collar that works on a similar principle to the Ultrasonic Anti-Barking Collar, but using a totally different method. This collar is also a deterrent, a stick rather than a carrot, and works by releasing the aroma of citronella, rather unpleasant to a dog, each time he barks. This spray is totally harmless, but teaches your dog that his barking has consequences which he would prefer to avoid.

Research has shown that the spray collar has successfully treated nuisance barking in over 80% of cases, but it should be borne in mind that it still needs to be used in partnership with a training method to reinforce its message. A dog will not necessarily associate the citronella smell with his barking unless this is backed up by the owner's command '(hush', or 'quiet') , as referred to earlier. As this is the case, there is no reason why the barking prevention methods described in a previous chapter should not be attempted first. They are free to use after all – apart from a large supply of treats!

I should also mention the Escalation Collars which are deemed to have a greater effect in the long run because they reward the dog for stopping barking sooner. The principle is to begin with a low level of noise – or a spray in the case of a citronella version – which gradually intensifies as the dog continues to bark. They are intended to teach the dog that he can stop barking before the unpleasantness increases, rather than put up with the full effect.

The jury is out on whether deterrent collars, in general, are a 'good thing', and I suppose this depends on whether or not you consider corporal punishment for children to be a 'good thing.' This is obviously more the case with electric shock collars, which are designed to transmit pain – however slight – to your dog. In the case of the 'unpleasant', rather than the painful, deterrent collars it is a judgment call which many dog owners would be very reluctant to make.

In my opinion, you should first try to examine the root cause of your dog's excessive barking and try to eliminate that cause through as many means as you have available. A long-term solution may need more time to be put into practice than a quick fix, but it will ultimately be more satisfying for you, and probably also for your dog if you can work out the problem together.

10. Dogmas

Tips to Remember:

OK, I'm all ears © Sue Byford

- Develop a training plan, and stick to it
- Be consistent in your training
- Behavior modification training takes practice. Repetition is the key, just like human learning 'parrot fashion'

- Do not reward barking behavior

But,

Give your dog an alternative to barking which he will enjoy even more.

Think like a dog – are you being consistent? Do you want him to bark as a deterrent to strangers coming near your house, then NOT bark when you don't want him to?

`Do you want me to bark or not?` © Bryan Schmidt Photography

Do you yell at your dog to shut up? Your dog has gained your attention, just as he wanted – and YOU are barking too. He thinks that he has established dominance over you because you are responding to his barking. That is reinforcement behavior in the wrong direction!

If you are leaving your dog alone and you know he responds to noises by barking, why not disconnect the phone – and even the doorbell – before you go out?

Boredom barking is something to watch out for, particularly in working breeds. Make sure your dog has plenty of exercise, and plenty of toys to play with if you are busy. Remember the mantra: bored dogs bark.

Reward your dog when he is NOT barking, especially if he has just stopped barking and become quiet. If he knows that being quiet brings a reward, what do you think he will choose to do?

You don't want a barking dog? Buy a Basenji.

11. Dog Breed Barking Characteristics

The American Kennel Club recognizes seven specific types of dog breed, and in many cases dogs within each breed type have similar barking characteristics.

Hounds

...the clue is in the name.

Hounds have been bred to cry out over quite long distances when their prey has been cornered. Consequently their barks can be rather loud, sometimes howling or baying. Think *Hound of the Baskervilles!*

Sporting Dogs

Sporting dogs require a significant amount of exercise (see boredom barking) and although their barking sounds are quite mixed, they may be candidates for barking training at some stage. Some sporting dogs: Pointers, Retrievers, Spaniels, Setters.

Working Dogs

These are mostly big breeds, with big voices. They can be prone to boredom barking. They may not necessarily bark often, but you will certainly know it when they do, as the deep, resonating bark starts to shake the ornaments off your neighbor's shelves! Some working dogs: Great Danes, Doberman, Rottweiler, Newfoundland, Schnauzer, Samoyed, Boxer.

Herding Breeds

These dogs are particularly known to bark at strangers, as they are bred with a highly tuned protective instinct.

Toy Dogs

Small dogs have small voices, though these can be quite penetrating over a short distance.

Terriers

Terriers are usually quite short, and their vocal chords are correspondingly short. This gives them a tendency to have yappy barks, and as a breed type they have a tendency to be excitable. Add these two together, and you have a potential recipe for some excessive barking going on!

Non-Sporting Dogs

These have no common denominator, being from very diverse backgrounds, and the type of barking will really depend on the individual temperament of your dog. Some non-sporting dogs: Dalmatian, Lhasa Apso, Poodle, Bulldog, Chow Chow

The Basenji

If you choose a basenji then he is the only non-barking breed you will find, although he won't be totally silent!

12. The Aftermath: Like A Dog With Two Tails!

The time you have spent reading through this book should be well rewarded, with your new-found control over a worrying aspect of your pet's behavior. In the past you may well have felt helpless in the face of a difficult situation which wears you down over time.

There can be little doubt that, when you have achieved success with the barking training described in this book, you will have proven undeniably that a positive outcome can be won through persistence and perseverance. There will be a spin-off from this in other areas too, as you will discover.

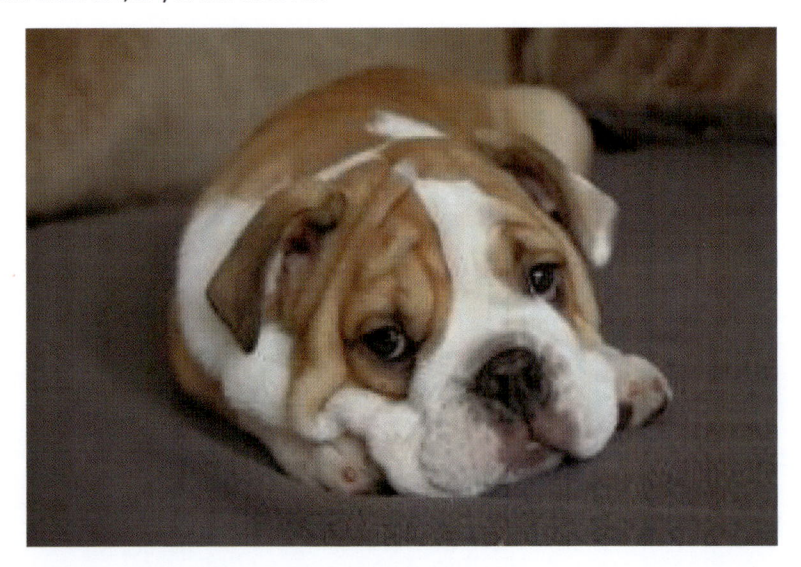

Now *we understand each other!* © Colin Hughes

What you will have done is to break a cycle which previously seemed beyond you, by discovering the cause and effect, determining an outcome in advance, then applying a process to achieve that outcome. A negative pattern of behavior will have been altered methodically and permanently.

If you have followed the steps properly then your life and your dog's life should be much more harmonious, with each other and with any other people involved (neighbors, for example). You could also apply several of these techniques, in adapted form, to other areas of your dog's life that can be improved.

Your new skills are also a power, which needs to be used carefully and responsibly. Remember that a dog is a dog, and you don't want a performing seal eating that dog food.

I just want to relax and be myself © Sarej

13. Photo Acknowledgements

Thank you to the following photographers for their valuable input to this book.

- *Howl* (cover photo and chapter headings), courtesy of Nazreth
- *There are so many things to bark about*, courtesy of Lilyz Studio
- *I'm going to be tired after all this running around*, courtesy of Asia Jones
- *Woof*, courtesy of Sue Byford
- *I can bark if you want*, courtesy of Lejla Alic
- *Four Puppies* , courtesy of Dani Gi
- *Natural noise and flamboyance*, courtesy of Aokiharu
- *Please play with me*, courtesy of Dimitri Castrique
- *Somewhere I can feel relaxed and contented*, courtesy of Mariana Figueroa
- *Was that the doorbell?* courtesy of Wookiee
- *Who keeps ringing that doorbell?* courtesy of Macej
- *Something to chew on*, courtesy of Cookai
- *Hidden Treasures*, courtesy of Kathyra1
- *Is that the mail man again?* courtesy of Daniel Andrés Forero
- *What's going on out there?* courtesy of Ned Horton
- *OK, I'm all ears*, courtesy of Sue Byford
- *Do you want me to bark or not?* courtesy of Bryan Schmidt Photography, Minneapolis
- *Now we understand each other*, courtesy of Colin Hughes
- *I just want to relax and be myself*, courtesy of Sarej

Listen While You Walk Your Dog!

Get the MP3 Audio Version here:

https://mydogwontstopbarking.com/audio/

Printed in Great Britain
by Amazon